pocket
cornwall

C000300316

Wild Looe

Derek Spooner

Alison Hodge

First published in 2014 by
Alison Hodge, 2 Clarence Place, Penzance,
Cornwall TR18 2QA, UK
info@alison-hodge.co.uk
www.alisonhodgepublishers.co.uk

ISBN-13 978-0-906720-94-3

British Library Cataloguing-in-Publication Data
A catalogue record for this book is available
from the British Library.

Designed and originated by
BDP – Book Development and Production
Penzance, Cornwall

Printed in China

Title page: A rabbit enjoys a summer evening
in the meadow

Photo credits

Photographs are reproduced on the pages
listed by kind permission of: David Chapman,
72 nuthatch; Martin Gregory, 54 whimbrel;
David Haines, 12 dolphin, basking shark, 35,
36; Christopher Halls, 52 grey mullet; Philip
Hambly, 1, 54 kingfisher, 66 emperor dragonfly,
67 roe deer, 72 great spotted woodpecker,
song thrush, 73 owl, 74 hairstreak, holly blue,
78 stoat, mole; Keith Hiscock, 16 lesser dogfish,
18 starfish; Adrian Langdon, 12 gannet, 23 black
redstart, 78 yellowhammer; Claire Lewis, 37
common seal; Paul Lightfoot, 8, 10–11, 14, 17,
20 top left, 22 top, 23 turnstone, 25 top, 26
wren, 31 top, 32 top, 39, 40, 41, 43 top, 44,
46, 47, 49, 50, 51, 53 top, 54 egret, 55, 56,
57, 58, 59, 60 bluebell, 62, 64–5, 76–7, 79
swallow and hedge, 80, 83 top, 87 left; Peter
McMurdie, 6 left, 60 orchid, 67 badgers, fox,
72 green woodpeckers, 83 jay, 86 hedgehog;
Robert Minchin, 38; Paul Naylor, 16 left; Matt
Nott, 15, 18 dahlia anemone; Sue Sayer, 32
middle; Matt Slater 18 crab, stalked jellyfish, 22
bottom; Christine Spooner, 12 seal, 13 left, 18
snakelocks anemone, 19, 25 bottom, 26 top,
45 all except bee, 52 top, 60 acorns, bilberry,
61, 66 left, 69, 74 fritillary and speckled wood,
79 primroses, 81 left, 85, 86 frog, spider, slow
worm, caterpillar; Derek Spooner, 4, 5, 6 right,
7, 13 right, 20 oystercatcher nesting, chicks, 28,
29, 30, 31 bottom, 32 bottom, 34, 37 right, 43
bottom, 53 bottom, 54 shelduck, 81 right, 82,
83 crow, 87 robin; Leon Truscott, 45 bee, 66
right, 74 moth, 86 moth; Wild Futures, 48.

Contents

Introduction: A Walk on the Wild Side

East Looe's Wooldown

I have the good fortune to live in the sub-urban area of a small East Cornwall coastal town – the Barbican area of Looe. To me the essential feature of life in Looe is my interaction with the natural world on my doorstep. Although I live in a town I am very conscious of the immediacy of the 'wild side' of Looe –

and I am not referring to the revellers who throng Fore Street on Saturday nights. Each day I renew acquaintance with the natural world as soon as I step into the street, and within a short distance of home is an exciting diversity of habitats.

A few metres away is the Wooldown, which I visit every morning with my dog, and

Looe Island from the Wooldown

my daily walk there serves to remind me of the biodiversity on offer. The Wooldown is an area of public access, owned by the people of Looe (through the East Looe Town Trust) – three fields plus fringing copse and hedgerow high above the busy streets of East Looe, a piece of Cornish countryside miraculously preserved within the town. At one time it was pasture for sheep and horses, but the grazing animals are long gone, and it is now heavily used by dog-walkers, visitors and local residents who come to sit and gaze out at the island and the ocean beyond.

It's mid-April, and as Scully and I enter the Wooldown I hear the insistent song of chiffchaffs resounding across the open fields. Magpies are chattering in the hedgerow, and I disturb a flock of linnets. A rabbit lopes leisurely into the hedge as Scully approaches.

I pause by the beacon to take in the view. Below me to the west I can glimpse the town and the river that bisects it; a noisy cloud of gulls rises over the rooftops. On the mud in the harbour I can see more gulls, doubtless scavenging for discards from the fish quay. Inland the valley sides are cloaked in oak woodland – Kilminorth and Trenant – still brown

Male bullfinch (left); male chaffinch and blackthorn (right)

and grey as winter fades. In front of me I can see the rocky shore off Hannafore and the familiar shape of Looe Island. Cormorants are drying their wings on the rocks beyond the Banjo Pier at the harbour entrance. To the south the Eddystone lighthouse is clearly visible on the horizon, about twelve miles offshore. Here I feel on the rim of a vast space. Beyond Looe Island a diagonal line south-west would make the next landfall the Azores in mid-Atlantic. I am standing on the edge of the ocean – the last great wilderness.

I begin my descent from the Wooldown, down a zigzag of tracks on to the Cornish coast path. I spot an early summer visitor, a whitethroat, just returned to its territory in the brambles, and hear the soft whistle of bullfinches and the churring of long-tailed tits – both are year-round hedgerow residents here. The blackthorn is already in glorious white bloom, and the hedge bottom is bursting with yellow-green alexanders, the delicate white flowers of three-cornered leeks and splashes of red campions. A chaffinch is pouring out its rollicking song from a perch in the blackthorn: 'Sweet will you will you kiss me dear'! Bumble bees are already active, and Scully flushes an early tortoiseshell butterfly from the nettles. My mind flashes back to those extraordinary weeks in 2009 when hundreds of painted ladies (invaders from North Africa) fluttered across the meadows,

Singing dunnock (left); red admirals on Wooldown ivy (right)

followed later in the year by swarms of red admirals feasting on the ivy.

The tide is out and I drop down to the East Looe beach. The black redstart that wintered by the gig house has gone; wrens and dunnocks are singing in the tangled scrub of the undercliff. I make my way east along the shore behind the exposed rocks of the Limmicks towards Plaidy. A little egret daintily picks its way through the rock pools. Thirty years ago a sighting of this bird would have meant a red-letter day; now they are commonplace. Several whimbrel rise from the beach; I hear their tittering calls before I see them.

I scan the surface of the sea, hoping to see a grey seal. There is a small population in the area, but today there are none in view. In the cove at Chough Rock the fulmar colony is indulging in noisy courtship rituals. The birds returned to the site in December and a few pairs will breed. Intermittently individual birds float off the cliff face and circle the cove in that stiff-winged glide that reminds us that they are not gulls but more closely related to albatrosses. Fulmars have only nested in Cornwall since the 1940s, and this site, one of only a handful along this coast, is most unusual in being located in an urban area.

Slowly I clamber back up the cliff. Then the dog and I head up the road for home, accompanied by the tinkling calls of goldfinches, and with an eye open for the house

Fulmar in flight

the principal habitats already introduced, and some of the fauna and flora that can be encountered in each. First, the sea and rocky shore, including Looe Island, with its bird colonies and seals; second, the maritime cliffs and grassland along the coast footpath; third, the estuary of the Looe rivers, with its intertidal mud flats and saltmarsh, and the other rivers that cross the area; fourth, the valley oak woodlands (in both the Looe and Seaton valleys); and finally, the rural hinterland, with its patchwork of farmland, hedgerows and hamlets. The account is based in large part on my experience over the last decade in wandering this 'home patch', binoculars and notebook in hand, and is biased towards the larger fauna.

Derek Spooner, 2014

sparrows nesting in the roofs of the villas that look out over the sea. My walk has lasted less than an hour, but it has reminded me of the proximity of the wild and the diversity of habitats encompassed here in a small area. I feel refreshed, my appetite whetted for further exploration of the wild side of Looe.

This description of Wild Looe centres on the town of Looe and the valleys of the Looe rivers. It also takes in the coast stretching west past Polperro to Lansallos and east to Downderry, plus a rural back country stretching out to villages like Lanreath, Pelynt and Widegates. I will describe in more detail

Abbreviations used in this book

ASNW	ancient semi-natural woodland
BAP	Biodiversity Action Plan
CSG	Cornwall Seal Group
CWT	Cornwall Wildlife Trust
LMCG	Looe Marine Conservation Group
LNR	Local Nature Reserve
MCZ	Marine Conservation Zone
NT	National Trust
SSSI	Site of Special Scientific Interest
VMCA	Voluntary Marine Conservation Area

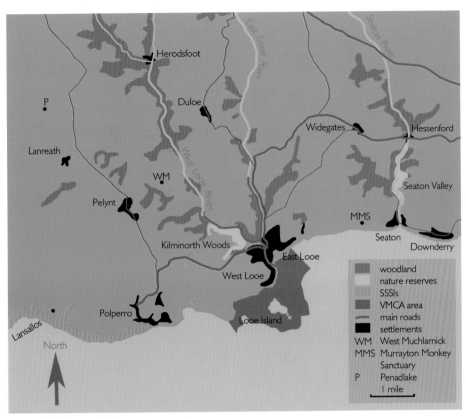

Herodsfoot

Duloe

Widegates

Hessenford

P

Lanreath

Seaton Valley

WM

MMS

Pelynt

Seaton

Downderry

Kilminorth Woods

East Looe

West Looe

Looe Island

Polperro

Lansallos

North

	woodland
	nature reserves
	SSSIs
	VMCA area
	main roads
	settlements
WM	West Muchlarnick
MMS	Murrayton Monkey
	Sanctuary
P	Penadlake
	1 mile

Map of the Looe and Polperro area

Sea and Rocky Shore

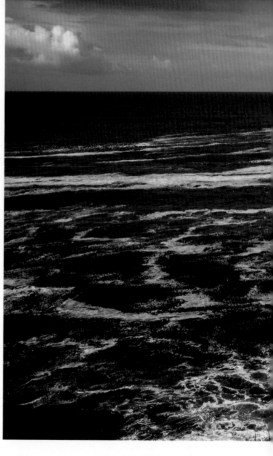

Mother, I hear the water
  Beneath the headland pinned,
And I can see the sea-gull
  Sliding down the wind.
I taste the salt upon my tongue
  As sweet as sweet can be.
Tell me, my dear, whose voice you hear?
  It is the sea, the sea.

('Tell Me, Tell Me, Sarah Jane', *I Had a Little Cat: Collected Poems for Children*, Macmillan, 2009)

These words by Cornish poet Charles Causley evoke for me the wildness of the Cornish coast, which is the natural starting point for our description of Wild Looe. Sit on a headland near Looe or Polperro and look out to sea, and you become aware of a wild and salty underwater world, familiar to the fisherman or the diver, but revealing itself only in glimpses to the land-based observer.

Sometimes the creatures of the open ocean do show themselves. This coast is visited by marine mammals, drawn by the fluctuating presence of shoals of fish. Grey seals are the most easily visible, but you may be lucky enough to see dolphins or porpoises, regular visitors to these waters. The most

frequent are common dolphins, but occasionally a small pod of the larger and rarer bottle-nosed dolphins – or a lone individual – appears in the bay, or you may be lucky enough to see an unusual visitor, like the white-beaked dolphin. Sadly cetacean corpses sometimes wash up on local beaches, including those of less common species – in re-

Clockwise from top: Gannet; white-beaked dolphin; basking shark in Looe harbour; grey seal

cent years there have been records of Risso's and striped dolphins. Also drawn by fish shoals is the gannet. This spectacular seabird can be seen at any time of year, despite the distance

Great northern diver in summer plumage (above); Looe's lone drake eider (right)

from any of its breeding colonies, the nearest of which are in the Channel Islands and Brittany. Gannets travel long distances to feed, and in winter disperse around the coast.

In summer, another magnificent visitor to this coast is the huge basking shark, the world's second largest fish. Its arrival is unpredictable, dictated by its food source, plankton, which blooms when sea conditions are favourable. In the summer of 2012, a basking shark swam into Looe harbour, but it would be more usual to see one drifting slowly past a local headland. Warming seas may mean that these extraordinary creatures move further north. More occasionally, a sunfish or even a turtle appears.

In winter, the inshore waters attract avian visitors from the north. Looe Bay and the sheltered waters between Hannafore and Looe Island are an excellent place to see great northern divers and Slavonian and great crested grebes. Further east, red-throated divers are commonly seen off Seaton and Murrayton — typically, in their winter plumage. In September 2008 a great northern diver that took up residence in Looe harbour was in full breeding plumage, providing a visual treat for local birders. Sea ducks are also less regular winter visitors, including eider. This large, heavy-billed duck feeds in shallow water by diving for crabs and other shellfish, and visits the south-west

Gulls follow a fishing boat into Polperro

in small numbers from northern Britain. In recent years one solitary drake eider has been marooned in Looe, frequenting the beaches and offshore rocks and consorting with gulls, conspicuous in its black and white breeding plumage. Why it has lingered here rather than returning to Northumberland or Scotland is not clear, but its presence is a delight.

The economy of Looe and Polperro is still closely linked to fishing, which exploits the resources of the wilderness offshore. The huge shoals of pilchards which were plundered in the past, and whose processing and storage shaped the backstreets of East Looe, are no more, but a small fleet of day boats still trawls for a wide variety of species, many of them shipped fresh to markets up country or on the continent. Smaller boats hand-line for mackerel, large shoals of which are often present close inshore in the spring, and crabs and lobsters are harvested from pots. In summer, recreational fishermen take boat trips seeking mackerel, bass and conger eels.

Looe also has a history as the country's major shark fishing centre and headquarters of the Shark Angling Club of Great Britain. In the 1950s and 1960s the day's biggest catch with its recorded weight was suspended on public view on the quayside. However, the huge decline in numbers of many shark species has thankfully led to a change in practice. Since 1994 the sharks that are caught (normally more than 12 miles out) are measured and tagged after capture and quickly returned to the sea alive, without being brought back to Looe. A variety of species is caught, with blues being most common; porbeagles and threshers are also captured.

This part of Cornwall has also been important in the development of the natural history of fishes. Polperro doctor Jonathan Couch was Cornwall's foremost naturalist in the nineteenth century. His leading speciality was ichthyology (the biology of fishes), and his observations and meticulous paintings of fish specimens brought to him by Polperro fishermen adorn his *History of British Fishes* published in the 1860s. Couch was a qualified medical doctor, but largely a self-taught naturalist. His *Journal of Natural History* and numerous other publications were based closely on his observations of the natural world within the locality. They provide an invaluable source of information about Wild Looe in the nineteenth century.

The seagrass meadow

The seagrass meadow

Hidden from sight on the sea floor a short distance from the shore in Looe Bay lies an important feature – an extensive 'meadow' of seagrass. This stretches from East Looe beach eastwards at least as far as Millendreath, and lies seaward of the Limmicks; there are smaller patches between Hanna-

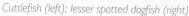
Cuttlefish (left); lesser spotted dogfish (right)

fore and Looe Island. The grass is common eelgrass (*zostera marina*), and unlike marine algae, it is a true flowering plant, with roots, leaves and rhizomes. It cannot survive in deep water due to light-limitation, and dies back in winter. The extent of the seagrass beds appears to reflect the sheltered nature of this area of Looe Bay. Seagrass meadows enhance the local biodiversity, and are recognized as a UK Biodiversity Action Plan (BAP) priority habitat. The grass provides shelter and a nursery for many species, some of which attach themselves to the grass, and also traps sediment and reduces coastal erosion. It is an important breeding ground for commercially important species of fish.

Among the inhabitants of the meadow are the two-spot goby, John Dory, greater pipefish, rock cook and corkwring wrasse, as well as cuttlefish and the netted dog-whelk that lays its eggs on the sea-grass fronds. The cuttlefish is not a fish but a true mollusc that lurks in the sandy seabed and uses its suckers to prey on other molluscs and small fish. It takes its name from its unique, porous, internal shell, the cuttle, which gives it buoyancy, and is often washed up on our beaches. The 'mermaid's purse' which contains the egg of a dogfish may be attached to the grass. The lesser spotted dogfish (or catshark) is common in these waters. Sadly there are no recent records of seahorses in the Looe seagrass beds, but local divers live in hope of finding them, as it is a favoured habitat for this elusive creature.

The rocky shore

Along the shore a plethora of wildlife can be found. Marine creatures have a varied ability to tolerate exposure to air and sunlight, and so different microhabitats develop different flora and fauna. The rocky reefs exposed at low tide are rich in intertidal species, and provide spawning grounds and hiding places for fish and crustaceans, whereas the higher areas of the shore are dominated by hardy creatures such as limpets, barnacles and sea snails that can sucker down and wait for the incoming tide. This is a rewarding coast for rock-pooling. Hannafore is perhaps the richest area, and is the most accessible, but there are also excellent pools that can be reached at low tide at Downderry, Seaton, Millendreath and the Limmicks off East Looe, and in Talland Bay. At Talland the remnants of the 1922 wreck of the French trawler *Marguerite* provide an additional structure that shelters marine life.

Each of these areas can provide subtly different concentrations of rock pool species. Most teem with shrimps, and lurking among the seaweed are small fish like the common

The rocky shore at low tide, Downderry

Facing page, clockwise from top left: Velvet swimming crab; spiny starfish and great grey sea slug; stalked jellyfish; dahlia anemone; snakelocks anemone. Above: Tompot blenny

blenny (also known as the shanny) and the Cornish clingfish. The largest British blenny, the tompot blenny, is found in crevices among the rocks below the low-tide line and may sometimes be seen guarding its nest.

The rocky reefs are home to a colourful range of anemones. These include the writhing snakelocks, beadlet (the commonest), gem, dahlia and strawberry anemones. Closely related to the anemones are the stalked jellyfish. Both use stinging cells within their tentacles to stun or kill prey, and as a means of defence against predators. Stalked jellyfish are effectively upside-down jellyfish with their tentacles on the top. They remain attached to seaweed or seagrass all their lives, but are mobile, rather like caterpillars. Four species of stalked jellyfish have been found in the vicinity of Looe.

Here too are a variety of beautiful starfish – often prey for the local gulls – sea urchins, sea squirts and sponges. The spiny starfish – much bigger than the common starfish – is particularly striking. Along the floor of the pools, beneath the abundant seaweeds and in rock crevices, scuttle a wide variety of

Oystercatchers. On the rocks and nesting (top left and right); chicks, newly hatched, and caught for ringing (above, left and right)

crabs, including the large edible crabs (sought by fishermen), with their familiar reddish-brown carapace, which can grow to more than 25 cm across. Another crab that can grow to a formidable size and is commercially exploited is the common spider crab. Here too are hermit crabs, which live inside the relict shells of dead molluscs. Masked crabs, which burrow in the sand, are found in the muddy sands at beaches like Millendreath.

Among the swimming crabs the largest is the velvet swimming crab – a voracious predator with vivid red eyes and a velvety shell. It is sometimes called the devil crab.

Another member of the swimming crab family is the much smaller and very numerous green shore crab. This is the crab sought in summer by scores of children on the harbour wall with lines and buckets.

The rocky shore is home to numerous molluscs, including top shells, limpets, dog-whelks and periwinkles, which have fleshy bodies often contained within a hard shell. These can endure exposure to the air, sunlight and variable temperatures when uncovered at low tide. Other members of the mollusc family, the sea slugs and sea hares, lack the hard shell. The tiny Celtic sea slug is found on Looe Island, and is a species largely confined to the far South West. Where the reefs extend into deeper areas there are forests of kelp, excellent cover for young fish and species like conger eel, cuckoo wrasse and pollack.

The abundance of potential prey is a magnet to many birds – gulls, of course, but also crows, which can sometimes be seen dropping molluscs on the rocks to break the shells, and, particularly evident, oyster-catchers. These birds are brash – noisy and colourful, with their black-and-white plumage (hence the name 'sea-pie'), orange-pink bill and legs. Oystercatchers do not feed on oysters, but on limpets, cockles, mussels and worms. In winter, flocks of oystercatchers are found along the shore at low tide, and in summer the less accessible rocky areas and beaches are home to breeding pairs. Oystercatchers make a minimal nest, relying on camouflage to keep it concealed. The young are born with their eyes open and capable of independent motion, and leave the nest within a few hours. They also rely on camouflage to avoid predators. Several pairs nest each year on Looe Island despite the abundance of gulls, and aggressively defend their nests and their young.

The strandline

On the beaches above the rocks is another important area for wildlife – the strandline. This is the deposit of seaweed and other debris left at the highest point of spring tides. The strandline is a fertile home for a host of invertebrates all year round, as a high temperature is reached inside the heaps of sea-weed – maggots, flies, sand hoppers, beetles and spiders flourish. Here you will find sea slaters – these are giant woodlice, which emerge at night when they are less vulnerable to predators, to feed on algae. Washed-

East Looe beach, showing the strandline and the rocky reefs of the Limmicks at low tide (above). Sea slater (left)

up items like cuttlefish bones, goose barnacles, mermaid's purses and whelk eggs are often found here. After autumn storms come wrecks of 'by-the-wind-sailors' – the dry transparent float and sails of pelagic hydroids. Succulent strandline plants may take root.

Where the strandline is allowed to develop free from interference, its abundance of

Turnstone

Female black redstart

potential prey makes it a magnet. It will be visited at night by rodents and flown along by hunting bats, while in the day it is attractive to birds. In winter there are relatively tame flocks of turnstones, visitors from the Arctic. Charles Causley, in his poem 'Turnstone', painted a neat picture of the bird:

Turnstone, tangle picker,
Sifting the ocean,
Wading the water,
Tipping the stone

They are sometimes joined by other waders like dunlins and ringed plovers. The strandline is a big attraction to pied wagtails and rock and meadow pipits, large numbers of which frequent the beaches, but it is also visited by garden birds, and by stonechats and black redstarts. The last are winter visitors to south-western coasts, and regularly take up residence at beaches like Millendreath and East Looe, where they position themselves on a rail and sally forth at intervals seeking their insect prey around the seaweed. In summer the main beach in East Looe is managed for human visitors and the seaweed is removed, but elsewhere it remains as an integral and vital component of beach ecology.

The Voluntary Marine Conservation Area and the Marine Conservation Zone

The particular qualities of the near-shore environment in Looe – clear water, diverse marine species – led in 1995 to the designation of the Looe Voluntary Marine Conservation Area (VMCA) by the local council, backed by conservation agencies. The area designated embraces almost 5 km of coastline from the Hore Stone in the west to the Limmicks in the east and the estuaries of the two Looe rivers to their tidal limit, plus Looe Island and the seabed and waters out to the 10-metre contour. The aims of the VMCA are to raise awareness of the marine environment; to encourage wise and sustainable use of its natural resources, and to support its biodiversity. Education and research into the local marine environment are important elements. Initially, the VMCA had little impact, but in 2007 Cornwall Wildlife Trust (CWT) embarked on a project based in Looe to reinvigorate the VMCA and to involve the local community.

This culminated in the establishment in 2012 of an independent Looe Marine Conservation Group (LMCG).

It must be stressed that the VMCA is indeed voluntary, and carries no extra statutory protection for its area. However, in 2013 the government announced the designation of ten Marine Conservation Zones (MCZs) in South West England, including one for 'Whitsand and Looe Bay', which includes the intertidal and subtidal habitats of the VMCA and stretches much further east to Rame Head. It includes the seagrass meadows and the plethora of habitats surrounding Looe Island Nature Reserve. While some details of the management regimes for MCZs remain to be resolved, the official recognition of the conservation importance of the area is highly welcome and a cause for celebration.

Looe Island

If there is one location in our area that encapsulates the notion of Wild Looe, it is the nine hectares of Looe Island, which lies less than a kilometre from the mainland, and is separated from it by a sheltered channel which on a few days a year is sufficiently shallow

Looe Island and Portnadler bay (above).
Crossing to Looe Island at extreme low tide (right)

to be crossed on foot at low tide. The island comprises a mixture of rocky cliffs, maritime grassland, scrub and woodland, with a shingle beach on the mainland side. There are three houses on the sheltered eastern side, with gardens and orchard. 'Little Island' to the south-east is joined to the main island by a footbridge, and further to the south-east lie

Hebridean sheep, Looe Island (above); wren (left)

the reefs and rocks of the Inner and Outer Ranneys. The summit of the island, at 47 m, provides commanding views over the sea and on a clear day west to the Lizard.

Until 2004, Looe Island was owned by the Atkins sisters, but on their death it was bequeathed to the CWT, who now manage it as a nature reserve. Two important tasks have been the eradication of rats and the restoration of the coastal grassland. Brown rats, thought to have come ashore from shipwrecks, have plagued the island for many years; Wilkie Collins described a great rat hunt (and subsequent 'rat and onions' feast!) when he visited Looe in 1850. Rats are a serious problem for ground-nesting birds, and when the Trust took over, the island was overrun. Successful eradication programmes have now been carried out, but rats are quite capable of swimming to the island, and continual vigilance is needed.

The problem of the island's grassland was that it was shrinking fast, due to the encroachment of scrub, especially bramble. This was diminishing the area available for nesting seabirds and attractive grassland plants, and making access difficult. A flock of around twenty hardy Hebridean sheep have been introduced, and once the undergrowth has been cleared their grazing prevents the scrub from recolonizing the grassland. These sheep are ideal in that they require relatively little maintenance apart from an annual shearing: they are nimble and foot-sure. Thrift, sea campion, spring squill, sea plantain and other grassland plants are on the increase,

and there are benefits for invertebrates and birds. Because the island has been largely spared from chemical applications it has excellent populations of butterflies and moths. The woodland is largely sycamore, but it is intended to increase its diversity by planting other native broad-leaved trees.

As with many islands, despite proximity to the mainland, physical separation has produced some ecological oddities. The only resident mammals appear to be bats, including lesser horseshoes, which find shelter in the woodland. There are some surprising absentees in the resident bird population. Since their arrival on the island in 2004, the wardens have yet to encounter a blue tit or a magpie – both common on the mainland. However, wrens are everywhere – at most times of year their loud and throbbing song is pervasive as they proclaim their territories, or if disturbed they emit a scolding rattle. Poet Ted Hughes described the wren as 'the burglar alarm of the undergrowth'.

Since 2004, over 80 bird species have been recorded. This includes a number of passage migrants, like whimbrel and bartailed godwit which appear regularly, and there are predators like heron, egret and peregrine which use the island as a hunting ground. The rocks of the Ranneys provide

Looe Island's cormorant colony (above); cormorant at nest (left)

an important haul-out for small numbers of grey seals.

The greatest significance of the island lies in its colonies of seabirds. It has the largest colony of great black-backed gulls in Cornwall, and large colonies of cormorants, shags and herring gulls, plus smaller numbers of fulmars and oystercatchers. All these species benefit from the lack of disturbance, and in summer parts of the island are out of bounds to visitors to protect the ground- and cliff-nesters.

Adult cormorant in breeding plumage (left); feeding time (above)

For cormorants and shags this is the most important breeding site in south-east Cornwall. Cormorants currently nest in a tight colony around the rim of a cove on the south-west side of the island; they nest early with as many as 30 pairs sitting on eggs in February (both male and female take turns at incubation), and many of the chicks fledged in April. By May the colony is crowded with young fledged birds loitering on the cliff and grassy slopes close to the nest sites. In spring the adults sport a distinctive white thigh patch and some have grey head markings, making them easy to distinguish from the smaller shags, with their handsome crests, green eyes and yellow beaks. On Looe Island the shags nest in similar numbers to cormorants but in a more scattered manner on ledges and in crevices nearer to sea level. Both species nest in small numbers at a few other sites on inaccessible cliffs between Talland Bay and Lansallos. Both feed by diving for fish. Cormorants are commonly seen inland, fishing in rivers and ponds several miles from the

Shags on Looe Island

sea (where they are not popular with fishermen), but shags are more exclusively maritime and rarely seen upstream of the main bridge in Looe.

Looe's gulls

If there is a bird that is emblematic of Wild Looe it is clearly the 'seagull', large numbers of which float in the skies over Looe and Polperro at all seasons; scavenge for food from sometimes unsuspecting visitors; nest on the roof-tops, to the annoyance of some local residents (but the pleasure of others); follow the fishing boats, and gather in noisy congregations on the sea-shore and the mud of the rivers at low tide. The townscapes of Looe and Polperro would be unimaginable without seagulls. Visitors are discouraged from feeding them by notices on the Looe quayside reminding them that 'THEY ARE VICIOUS', but these signs are often ignored by both gulls and visitors, sometimes with unfortunate consequences!

'Seagull' is not a species name. The familiar gull in Looe and Polperro is the herring gull, with grey back, pink legs, and yellow beak with a red spot. Since 1970 the number of herring gulls in the UK has fallen by 40 per cent (the bird is now 'red-listed' as of highest conservation priority), but this is not apparent in Looe, where hundreds of the birds are present throughout the year. Herring gulls are omnivorous and have adapted to urban living. In Looe and Polperro they nest in large numbers on buildings of all ages. Because they are noisy and dirty, some residents take measures to deter the birds from building nests, which can be quite large structures, but it is illegal to intentionally disturb or destroy the *active* nest of *any* wild bird. The eggs are laid in April/May, and in summer the plaintive cries of the brown juveniles begging for food are a familiar sound. The parent birds may dive bomb passing people and pets, though they rarely make physical contact. Chicks sometimes fall from the roofs, and may then be fed on the ground by the adults. Herring gulls are naturally cliff nesters, and there is a substantial colony on Looe Island, with around 80 pairs, plus a scatter of nests on the less accessible stretches of mainland cliff. In winter, numbers swell with an influx from other areas, including some continental birds.

Rooftop herring gulls (top). Herring gull and chick (above)

Unlike the herring gull, Looe's other breeding gull, the great black-back, does not usually build on roofs, but has a major colony on Looe Island. This is a magnificent bird, the largest species of gull in the world. The Looe Island colony, where there are currently over 70 nesting pairs, is now the largest in Cornwall. The great black-backed gull is the least common of the five major species that nest in the UK (with only about 2,000 pairs in England), though the population more than trebles in winter. These birds have flesh-coloured legs, yellow beaks, and jet-black backs. Great black-backs are nearly twice the size of herring gulls at maturity, and are intimidating predators, with fearsome beaks. As well as scavenging and robbing other birds of their prey, they will kill and consume other birds and mammals (up to the size of a puffin), and sometimes are cannibalistic. A good place to see them bullying other gulls is the Looe river by the fish quay, where birds gather to feed on the discards from the fishing boats.

On Looe Island black-backs nest predominantly in two areas of tussocky grassland above the cliffs – Little Island in the south-east

Great black-backed gulls. From top: adult in flight; chicks – a study in camouflage; chick being ringed

corner, and the sloping ledge in the south-west of the island. Our knowledge of the dynamics of the Looe Island colony is being enhanced by a ringing project, begun in 2010, led by local ornithologist Bruce Taggart. By ringing great black-back chicks each summer for at least five years, it is hoped to gain insights into the birds' ecology and life histories.

Ringing of the chicks takes place mainly in June when they are about a month old – not always the easiest process as the young birds have vicious beaks and can be quite feisty! They conceal themselves surprisingly well in the grass and sea beet, or among the grey rocks. They are collected in bags, ringed on both legs, and returned to the places where they were found. On the right leg is a white plastic ring with red lettering, legible with binoculars or telescope. The Looe rings carry a four-digit code, comprising three letters and a number (e.g. L:AF5). On the left leg is a metal British Trust for Ornithology ring.

In the first four years of the project over 230 chicks were ringed, though the numbers varied considerably from year to year. In 2012, cold and wet June weather led to high mortality in the colony. Although over 90 nests with eggs had been counted in May, only 25 chicks were found for ringing a month later.

Already records submitted by birders are showing where the young birds go. Great black-backs take three years to reach maturity (in which period they retain the brown juvenile plumage), so we do not know yet if the Looe birds will return to the island to breed, although it seems likely. Birds from the 2010 and 2011 contingents have been spotted in France, Wales, Hampshire, Guernsey and other parts of Cornwall, and many of them are seen in Looe, on the river or the island. The furthest location so far is north-west Spain. Some birds seen in Looe have returned after visits to the Channel Islands. But birds born and ringed in France or the Channel Islands can also be found in the Looe area in winter.

While the familiar herring gull and the spectacular black-backs are the only two breeding gull species in the Looe area, in winter they are joined by other species. The smaller, more delicate black-headed gulls (lacking their dark heads in winter) are common; this species breeds inland on Bodmin Moor. There are regular sightings of small numbers of the much rarer Mediterranean gull, particularly on Hannafore. Lesser black-backs (similar in size to the herring gull) are sometimes present.

The seals of Looe

'Nelson' and Looe's Banjo Pier

The only public statue in Looe is to Nelson – not the famous admiral, but his namesake, the large one-eyed male grey seal that frequented the harbour for several years. The statue is on Pennyland, opposite the lifeboat station. Nelson was obviously attracted by the prospect of free fish suppers from the local fishing boats. He died in 2003.

If you are fortunate, you *might* see a seal from any point on the mainland shore, but the most likely place to see them is off Looe Island. Since 2008 local volunteers, led by Sue Sayer from the Cornwall Seal Group (CSG), have been carrying out research into Looe's seal colony, aided by the Island's wardens, and an interesting picture is emerging.

The research project is based upon monthly visits to the island by a survey team, who count and photograph the seals. Identification of individual seals using digital photographic techniques is the key feature, with the possibility of linking to the database developed by the CSG, which includes over 800 individual seals. Every seal has a unique fur pattern, which it retains throughout its adult life, making it possible, with practice, to identify individuals. The photographic data is supplemented by pictures taken by the island wardens and by visitors.

Britain has two species of seal, the common (or harbour) seal and the larger grey (or Atlantic) seal. The seal normally seen in Cornwall is the grey seal, the largest British mammal that gives birth on land. This beautiful animal spends much of its time in the water, but hauls out regularly (especially at low tide) to rest and digest its food. The prime site in the Looe area used by seals to haul out is the group of rocks known as the Outer Ranneys, off the south-east corner of the island, and submerged at high tide. Seals are seen frequently in the water in the wild area on the south side of the Island.

Compared with some beaches in North Cornwall, or the Isles of Scilly, where over 100 seals may congregate, the numbers of

Snowdrop

Pawprint

Duchess

Lucille

Looe's seal regulars, hauled out on the Outer Ranneys in 2012

seals seen on Looe Island are tiny, with a maximum of eight individuals recorded on one day – in most months there are typically three or four seals present. A seasonal pattern has emerged. There are two peaks in numbers each year, the first coming in the spring moult, and the second within the summer offshore foraging season. Numbers decline in the autumn and early winter during the pupping season.

Photo identification has revealed that a large number of different seals visit Looe; by

'Lucille', a young female grey seal

2014 over 50 different individuals had been identified. The majority of these are transient – especially the males – many identified only once. Grey seals travel large distances, and many move between different sites in South West England, including the Isles of Scilly, and further afield to Wales and probably France and Ireland.

However, a few seals have shown strong site fidelity, staying at the Looe site for long periods. There have been at least 20 repeat visitors, and four adult females have been seen many times. 'Duchess' is easily recognizable as she is, like the famous Nelson, blind in one eye. 'Duchess' and another female, 'Snowdrop' have both been identified more than 150 times over a five-year period. These sightings have all been in the period

December to August. Intriguingly, each summer Snowdrop appears to be pregnant, and departs Looe Island for an unknown pupping site elsewhere. Early in 2011 she was seen several times at a haul-out in the Roseland peninsula. Two other regular females ('Pawprint' and 'Lucille') behave similarly, and have been seen in the winter pupping season among large haul-outs on the north coast near St Ives. Lucille, a young female popular with local boat operators, was seen frequently in August 2012 off Looe, but appeared, heavily pregnant, on a north coast beach in mid-October! She probably had her pup in North Cornwall or even South Wales. There is an identifiable seasonal gender pattern. In spring and summer females predominate, leaving the area in the autumn to pup elsewhere. In the autumn, males predominate and this continues through the winter months when numbers are low. Juveniles may be present at any time of year. Overall a picture has emerged of a small, fluid group, some of which visit Looe for months at a time, while many others stay only briefly.

An intriguing question is whether or not grey seal pups are born in the Looe area. Seals like secluded beaches with caves for pupping, and many find the conditions they need in West or North Cornwall. However,

Common (or harbour) seal, Looe Island (left). Grey seal pup, Hannafore beach, January 2014 (right)

weaned pups do turn up occasionally in the Looe area (the mother abandons the pup to fend for itself when it is three weeks old). In late 2009, three were found on the shore at Polperro, Hannafore and East Looe. These all appeared to be less than ten weeks old. In November 2010, a weaned seal pup was rescued at Downderry, and removed to the National Seal Sanctuary at Gweek, to prepare for release back into the wild. In the severe storms of early 2014 a seven-week pup was found resting on the beach at Hannafore, and another, probably a little older, appeared briefly on a flooded West Looe Quay before heading back to sea! But even young seal pups can travel long distances quite rapidly, so there can be no certainty where these seals were born.

Seals retain the ability to surprise. One morning, island warden Claire Lewis looked out from her cottage and saw a beautiful common seal stretched out on the rocks below her. This was only the fifteenth record of this species in Cornwall.

The studies of Looe's seals reveal a small and potentially fragile colony, with pregnant females in summer, clearly linked to larger colonies elsewhere. It is vital to the well-being of Looe's seals that they are treated with respect. They are wild predatory animals that need to be free from disturbance during their visits to Looe Island, and it is important that those who go out on the water to see them keep their distance.

The Cliffs and the Coast Path

Adder at Lansallos

Along the coast from Downderry to Lansallos runs a section of the great South Western coast path. It provides countless opportunities for scanning the sea for dolphins, seals and seabirds, and is an important component of the wild in its own right. Apart from the towns of Looe and Polperro, the coast is mostly devoid of settlement and the path takes a course between grassland and the overgrown tangle of vegetation along the cliffs which provides a habitat for many wild creatures. Large sections of the coast are owned and managed by the National Trust (NT), notably at the Struddicks near Sea-

ton, Hendersick west of Looe, and between Polperro and Lansallos. Some of the grassland is grazed by livestock owned by tenant farmers; the relative absence of chemical applications allows a wide range of plant species to flourish, supporting in turn a wide range of insects. The coast path is the best place in the area to see lizards and adders, which can sometimes be found basking in the summer sunshine. The beautifully marked adder is Britain's only poisonous snake, though the bite is seldom fatal to people; its favourite prey is in fact its relative, the common or viviparous lizard. Both lizards and adders hibernate in winter.

Geologically, most of the coast is dominated by Dartmouth slates, usually greenish or purplish in colour, sometimes red, violet or buff and much folded and faulted. Talland Bay displays some particularly fine examples of these variegated colours. East of the fault-line that runs through Portnadler Bay, the grits and grey slates of the Meadfoot beds, interbedded with thin limestone bands, reach the coast at Looe, Plaidy and Millendreath. These beds are also colourful and contorted, and

Dartmouth slates and head deposits make a colourful scene in Talland Bay

contain numerous fossils, often so flattened as to be difficult to identify. Fine examples of these greatly disturbed strata can be seen between Looe and Millendreath beaches.

West of Polperro the coastal strip has been designated a Site of Special Scientific Interest (SSSI), largely on account of its maritime hard cliffs, with interesting plant communities, backed by species-rich grassland, much of it unimproved. The assemblage of plants includes many scarce species, such as shore dock, sea knotgrass, slender bird's-foot trefoil and lanceolate spleenwort. The path in this section (and east to Portnadler Bay) is strongly undulating and traverses a series of coombes – minor valleys with tumbling small streams, sometimes with little waterfalls, where the coast has been cut back by the

Lansallos beach and cliff: part of an SSSI (left).
Portnadler beach: the effect of landslips (top);
slumping and low cliffs of 'head' deposits (above)

sea. In places the path crosses areas of head deposits (known locally as 'ram') – on slopes formed under tundra-like conditions. Head deposits are generally composed of a clay matrix containing angular rock fragments, and may overlie 'raised beaches' formed when the seal level was higher than it is today.

These areas are prone to landslips after periods of heavy rain – the bad weather of the winters of 2012–13 and 2013–14 saturated the ground and triggered a series of slippages along the cliffs, causing the path to be temporarily closed in places.

Some of the coombes have marshy floors or are partly wooded (West Coombe below Lansallos and East Coombe are good examples); others are given over to brakes of bramble and gorse (notably below Port Looe). At Lansallos a beautiful sunken green lane runs down to the beach; it was once used by farm carts to collect sand and seaweed from the beach, and, more excitingly, by smugglers. In the past the gorse – usually known as 'furze' – provided local farmers with an important source of fuel. The invasive gorse and bracken today is also extensive on the Struddicks and Hendersick, and on Lansallos Cliff; periodically areas are cleared for grazing or as firebreaks, but it provides suitable habitat for several important species of butterfly and bird, and cover for foxes and rabbits. Management of the grassland by the NT around Lansallos is aided by the grazing of hardy Dartmoor ponies or Dexter cattle brought in for the purpose. A curiosity both east and west of Polperro is the remains of old allotments with several exotic hedge species, especially veronica and escallonia. These luxuriant evergreen plants provided year-round shelter from the wind. Few of the allotments remain in use, and these overgrown areas now provide ample cover for wildlife.

In spring and summer the footpath is a riot of colourful flowers – sea thrift, wild thyme, field scabious, red campion, wild leeks, bluebells and many more. The path is outstanding for its butterflies. The rarest you are likely to find is the pearl-bordered fritillary – a UK BAP priority species – found near Murrayton and Lansallos. This butterfly has the black and orange pattern typical of fritillaries, and takes its name from the silvery spots, edged with brown, on the outer margin of the underside of the hindwing. The female lays her eggs on violets in dry, bracken-dominated habitats. This butterfly is on the wing for only a few weeks in early summer. Another relatively uncommon and tiny butterfly, easily overlooked, is the green hairstreak. Its green underwings provide excellent camouflage. Gorse is one of its foodplants. The path by Portnadler Bay is an excellent place to see butterflies, as is Lansallos Cliff, with small coppers, common and holly blues, gatekeepers and ringlets among those that thrive there. The footpath is also notable for the variety

and number of moths that can be found, including some day-flying species like the six-spot burnet. Rare Cornish coastal specialists include Barrett's marbled coronet, found on coastal cliffs, and the black-banded moth, found principally on food-plants splashed at high tide. A much commoner moth is the lackey, whose caterpillars may be found in mid-summer basking in extraordinary clustered ball-shaped webs. Other unusual insects can be found along this coast: hornet robberflies have been seen in several places,

East Coombe (top); its Dartmoor ponies (above)

including Talland Bay and Lansallos, and a recent colonist to Britain, the ivy bee, has spread west along the coast during the early

Spring flowers by the coast path near Polperro

years of this century. Also found at Lansallos and on the cliffs below the Wooldown in East Looe is the rare long-horned mining bee, another BAP priority species present at only a handful of Cornish sites. This solitary bee with distinctive long antennae lives in holes in the cliff and forages on flowers of the pea family.

The gorse and scrub along the path is home to several interesting species of birds.

A year-round resident is the jaunty stonechat; the chocolate-headed male is usually seen perched on a vantage point from which it can sally forth hawking for insects. The female is less colourful but equally active. In winter, stonechats sometimes move to the beaches, where they look for insects along the strandline. A more elusive, year-round resident is the Dartford warbler. It rarely shows itself for

Clockwise from top left: Pearl-bordered fritillary, under- and upperwings; green hairstreaks; ivy bee; lackey moth caterpillars; small copper

Male and female stonechats (above left and right); whitethroat (left)

long, spending most of its life skulking in the undergrowth. 'Stay-at-home/Never-roam/ Dartford warbler/Hiding in furze,' as Charles Causley put it in his poem 'Dartford Warbler'. However, on a warm, still day you may be lucky enough to encounter one perched on a gorse sprig – instantly recognizable by the long cocked tail which gives it a lop-sided appearance – and hear its brief, rattling song.

In summer, whitethroats arrive, and their noisy song flights make them conspicuous along the coast path. Other breeding birds in this grassland habitat include linnets, meadow pipits and skylarks. In spring, the enchanting songs of skylarks floating high above Hendersick mix with the raucous cries of gulls along the coast path from Looe to Talland.

The fescue grassland along the coast path is grazed by sheep and rabbits, and the latter attract plenty of predators. Foxes are a frequent sight and overhead buzzards circle. Buzzards are the commonest bird of prey throughout south-east Cornwall. Two others are seen frequently on the coast path. Kestrels nest regularly on the cliffs, and can sometimes be seen hanging in their classic 'windhover' pose. Sit a while on a headland and you have

Kestrel (left); buzzard (right)

a reasonable chance of seeing a passing peregrine, which also breeds on cliffs along this coast and ranges widely in its hunt for prey.

The Monkey Sanctuary

The coast path between Seaton and Millendreath is a challenging walk, with some steep climbs and great views across Looe Bay and east to the Rame Peninsula. Close to the footpath at Murrayton, in a patch of sycamore and beech woodland, is hidden another element of Wild Looe – the Monkey Sanctuary, established by Len Williams in 1964, and now a beacon for conservation not just in Cornwall but in a much wider world. Initially the sanctuary was a refuge for woolly monkeys rescued from the pet trade, and it established a breeding population of this beautiful South American primate, with a view to returning animals to the wild. Through time it has widened to take on the rescue of other primate species, particularly capuchins and Barbary macaques. Since its opening it has housed over 150 individual monkeys, living in social groups in specially designed territories. As the realistic chances of release to the wild receded, the breeding programme was abandoned in 2001.

Woolly monkey exploring Murrayton woodland

on all these issues. The Monkey Sanctuary remains the core activity of the charity now known as Wild Futures.

The site is also of interest for the beautiful gardens and woodland in which it is set. The old house and its outbuildings are home not just to monkeys but also to jackdaws and swallows; bullfinches, nuthatches and woodpeckers nest in the surrounding woodland; in the cellar of the house is a roost of lesser horseshoe bats, which can be viewed on closed-circuit television, and which forage in the area. The grounds are managed to demonstrate a range of techniques for encouraging wildlife, with a wide range of attractive native plants, including relative rarities such as slender and hairy bird's-foot trefoil. Murrayton is a special place.

The sanctuary's mission has significantly broadened through time. It is a leader in the field of primate welfare and conservation, but also engages in environmental education and in local wildlife management, and campaigns

Estuary and River

Between the Tamar and the Fowey rivers there is only one estuary, that of the Looe rivers, which enters the sea at the town of Looe. A short distance above Looe's only bridge the estuary bifurcates; the West Looe river is tidal for about two miles to beyond Watergate, and the East Looe for a similar distance, to Sandplace.

The river valleys here are the product of fluvial erosion, but have been inundated by the sea when the sea level rose at the end of the Devensian glaciation, about 12,000 years ago. Such drowned river valleys are known as rias. The Looe ria took approximately its present shape about 6,000 years ago, though human activity – the construction of towns and railway – has led to considerable land reclamation around the fringes of the estuary. The most obvious recent reclamation was in the 1970s, to construct Millpool car-park, the filling in of the large water area originally impounded to serve Looe's tide mill, but there has been minor accretion in many places.

Smaller river valleys to the west and east at Polperro, Millendreath and Seaton lack estuarial features; at Seaton the construction of a

The drowned valley of Looe with the town of East Looe built on reclaimed land

shingle beach by longshore drift across the valley entrance has enabled the Seaton river to make a small flood plain in its lower reaches.

It is easy to underestimate the importance of the estuary to the area as a natural resource. The twice-daily alternation and mixing of fresh and salt water with the tides provides a rich environment for many species. At the inland end of the tidal area are small areas of salt-marsh, flooded by spring tides. These are highly productive ecological areas, supporting a specialist range of salt-tolerant plants like common scurvy grass and sea

Morning mist on the salt-marsh of the West Looe river

purslane that can cope with the tidal inundation. The inter-tidal areas of mud and sand are home to important colonies of microscopic plants, bacteria and invertebrates, vital to the degradation and recycling of nutrients, and themselves the prey of fish, water birds, and fishermen digging for bait. Mudflats are classified in the UK as a BAP priority habitat worthy of special protection.

Fish

Among the bigger fish, salmon and sea-trout both travel up the estuary into the freshwater stretches of the rivers, with sea-trout in particular often sought by anglers. Testimony to the presence of these fish in the West Looe

The West Looe river at low tide (above). Yellow flag irises in the valley (right)

river is provided by the ancient construction of a fish-trap and weir-house near Trelawne Mill at Shallow Pool, just below the highest point of ordinary tides. The walled channel of the diverted river remains clearly visible to this day, with the old course of the river also still evident. The marshy area of the valley alongside the river here has wonderful displays of marsh marigolds and yellow irises

European eel (top). Grey mullet (above)

is not a separate species but an anadramous form of the freshwater brown trout, which migrates to the ocean for much of its life, returning to fresh water to spawn. Brown trout are found in the freshwater stretches of the Looe rivers.

There are other fish in these rivers that move between estuary and sea. The European eel, a BAP species, is sometimes encountered, though much rarer than in the past. European eel populations are thought to have declined by 95 per cent since the late 1980s, and the species is now classified as Critically Endangered. Eels have extraordinary lives: they travel 4,000 miles to the Sargasso Sea to breed, and tiny juveniles take five years to reach our rivers. They have suffered from habitat loss, pollution, over-fishing, and climate change affecting oceanic currents.

Grey mullet are common in the coastal waters; in summer, large shoals of these deposit-feeders move through the harbour into the estuary, and are clearly visible just as the tide begins to flood. The flounder is a flatfish that divides its time between estuaries and the sea, and is frequently prey for wading birds like egrets and divers like cormorants. The bass is another common species in the coastal waters, and its young spend their first four or five years in the estuary. The harbour walls

every spring. Shallow Pool was Cornish writer Geoffrey Grigson's favourite fishing pool. He describes how, in July 1925, he fished for seven nights for a total of eight sea-trout at Shallow Pool, though he failed to catch the much rarer salmon. Grigson referred to the sea-trout by the old West Country name of 'peal'. Sea-trout can still be seen in the deep pools of this stretch of the river. The sea-trout

and boat moorings are important in providing sites for barnacles, limpets and seaweed, and at the mouth of the estuary clusters of mussels can filter food from the fast-moving water. Look beneath Looe's only bridge at low tide and you will see mussel beds.

Birds and mammals

The estuary of the Looe rivers does not attract the large flocks of waders found on bigger Cornish estuaries like the Tamar, but it is home to some significant species. Pre-eminent is the grey heron, a large, long-legged bird with powerful bill capable of impaling fish and quite capable of consuming other birds' chicks and small mammals. For many years Trenant Woods has been home to one of the most visible small heronries in Britain, immediately opposite the Millpool car-park, thronged by visitors in summer. Herons usually nest colonially, and each year up to ten large nests are built in a tree at the water's edge, with large and noisy chicks easily visible and audible by April before the trees are thick with leaves. This is the only heronry between the Lynher and Fowey rivers. But herons can be seen striding in the shallows throughout

Grey herons in the Trenant heronry (top). Their chicks on a nest (above)

Clockwise from top left: Little egret; whimbrel; kingfisher; shelduck

the estuary system, as well as fishing in rock pools on the seashore or the Island.

Since the early years of the twenty-first century, the herons have acquired some neighbours. Their smaller cousin, the little egret, rarely seen anywhere in Britain before 1990, has moved in from the Continent. Little egrets first nested in the UK in 1996 in Dorset; now there are many colonies, and the birds are a common sight, easily identifiable by their all-white plumage, black legs and beak and bright yellow feet, which give them the appearance of having been dipped in custard. The white plumes on the head are a reminder that this species was almost a casualty of the millinery trade, with the plumes

The West Looe river near Sowden's Bridge

in heavy demand in the nineteenth century for ladies' hats. The plumage trade was a key factor in the founding of the Royal Society for the Protection of Birds (RSPB) in 1889, and thankfully the trade in plumage was banned in 1921. In Looe egrets nest primarily in the same tree as the herons, with an element of 'time-share' as the egrets nest later than their bigger relatives. In autumn and winter, numbers are supplemented by continental birds, and egrets are actually more numerous than herons around the estuary, with roosts of as many as 30 birds.

Other (non-breeding) wading birds on the estuary include oystercatchers, curlews and redshanks. In spring and autumn, flocks

River Seaton

records kept by local birders indicate that the numbers of wintering waders are significantly lower than in the 1990s, when sometimes flocks of over 100 curlew graced the mud-flats. Now it is unusual to find more than twenty. This is likely to reflect a wider decline in the population as much as any deterioration in local conditions.

There are other breeding birds on these rivers. In spring, a few families of shelduck appear on the estuary. They feed primarily on the tiny snails that lie on the surface of the mud. These spectacular large ducks nest in burrows on the valley sides before leading their ducklings down on to the river to run the gauntlet of crows, gulls and herons. Canada geese and mute swans are also residents, with large flocks of Canadas a familiar sight flying above the town in the autumn. In winter, little grebes are frequent visitors to the estuary, while moorhens and mallards are common throughout the year on ponds and rivers, including those at Seaton valley.

But the most spectacular resident is the kingfisher, which breeds most years on both the Looe and Seaton rivers. The easiest place to see kingfishers is on the estuary in late summer at low tide when the shallow water makes easier fishing. At this time young birds have begun to disperse after the breed-

of whimbrel pass through, stopping off on the seashore as well as the estuarine mud. The tittering of whimbrel passing overhead is a familiar sound. Occasionally a greenshank turns up, and common sandpipers bob at the river's edge during their passage. Sadly,

ing season. In winter, birds also visit the rocky shore in the search for food. The kingfisher is a small bird, not much bigger than a sparrow, and, despite the bright colours, it is surprisingly invisible when stationary on a favoured perch; the flash of blue and piping whistle as it darts away betray its presence.

Upstream of the tidal limits or on the Seaton or Pol, water birds are fewer, although you may be lucky enough to see a dipper. But the quintessential bird of these stretches is the grey wagtail. When Geoffrey Grigson was growing up in Pelynt before the Second World War, he considered this beautiful bird, grey with yellow underparts, one of the 'eminent species of the parish' – 'there is no parish where you could study him more easily or find in a small compass a larger population'. Grey wagtails are found in scattered pairs on small, fast-flowing streams with plenty of exposed rocks and pebbles, and in winter may visit the estuary or sea-shore. Their bouncing flight and lively 'zi-zi' call makes them easy to spot along the rivers, yet trippers trudging down from the Polperro car-park to the harbour often seem unaware that these lovely wagtails as well as dippers are bobbing on the rocks in the River Pol beside the road.

Other creatures find their prey in the riverine environment. Cornwall is one of the UK's

Grey wagtail

strongholds for the otter, and there are regular reports of otters in the Looe and Seaton rivers, though individual animals have large territories and they are difficult to see. Telltale 'spraints', or footprints in the mud, are often the only evidence of their presence. Otters also visit smaller streams and ponds during their nocturnal wanderings, and occasionally turn up in surprising places. A villager in Nomansland was astonished to see, on a night camera, an otter visiting her garden pond. Sad to say, her pond is no longer stocked with carp!

The Valley Woodlands

Ancient semi-natural woodland alongside the West Looe river

A crucial contributor to the biodiversity of Wild Looe is the presence of ancient woodland along the river valleys. This is particularly significant in the landscape of the West Looe valley, where Kilminorth and Trenant Woods face each other across the tidal waters of the estuary, but ancient woodland is also present intermittently alongside the East Looe river,

Autumn colours in Kilminorth and Trenant Woods

and in the Seaton Valley, sometimes interspersed with other broad-leaved woodland. The woodland is usually backed by pastoral farmland on the less steep ground away from the valley sides. These woods form some of the best preserved and most extensive examples of ancient woodland in Cornwall, and most have public access. The woods clothe the steep slopes of the river valleys with a colourful carpet, green in spring and summer, brown and yellow in autumn, and provide a beautiful backdrop to the urban landscape of Looe. Cornwall is one of the few places where ancient woodland meets the tidewater.

It would be a mistake, though, to think of such woods as some sort of pristine, prime-

Clockwise from top left: Sessile oak acorns; bluebell; early purple orchid; bilberry flower

val wilderness, or 'wildwood'. As woodland historian Oliver Rackham has pointed out, this ceased to exist in Britain in the Neolithic period (or before). These valley woods are properly defined as 'ancient semi-natural' woodland (ASNW). This description reflects their antiquity – woodland has been continu-ously present for at least 400 years – but also the fact that they have been modified by people over the centuries, particularly through the practice of coppicing. This continued in the area until the 1950s; its impact can be seen clearly in the character and structure of the woodland. The woods are also described as 'upland oak woods', a habitat type defined less by altitude than by location and species composition. The dominant species is the western or sessile oak, but beech is also fre-quently present, planted especially along the main bridle paths, and there are locally signifi-cant numbers of birch, sweet chestnut and sycamore (the last two non-native species in Cornwall), plus the occasional ash, wild cherry or large conifer. Sessile oak (*Quercus petraea*) can be distinguished from its pedun-culate lowland cousin (*Quercus robur*) by its stalkless acorns.

Left to right: Porcelain fungus; honey fungus; amethyst deceiver

The practice of coppicing involves the cutting down of the young trees every few years at near ground level, to use for timber or charcoal, and allowing the trees to regrow by sprouting shoots from the 'stool' that is left. The coppiced trees, mainly oak, tend to be closely spaced with relatively straight trunks, rather narrow in girth. The result is a closed canopy, and in summer the woodland is heavily shaded. In much of this woodland there is an understorey of holly and, less commonly, hazel. The combined effect is a fairly sparse ground flora. The woods are characterized by an abundance of bryophytes – mosses and liverworts – especially on hedge banks and fallen logs as well as the trees themselves, contributing to the lush, verdant atmosphere. Ferns add to the luxuri-

ance in summer. Dead timber, upright and fallen, is common, providing excellent nest sites for birds and mammals, and homes for countless invertebrates. A healthy wood with high biodiversity needs plenty of dead trees!

Within the woods there are few clearings, but where trees have fallen, and along the rides and paths, more light penetrates to the floor and the ground flora is more diverse, with plenty of bramble, bilberry and common cow-wheat, and better conditions for butterflies and other invertebrates. The soils are shallow and acidic, and this is reflected in the vegetation. In spring, parts of the woodland see a glorious flourishing of woodland flowers – bluebells, wood anemones and primroses, wood sorrel and early purple orchids. In autumn, the fungi come

There are also invasive species – presenting potential management problems. In some places rhododendron is a threat; it outcompetes native plants, leading to a decline in habitat quality. Eradication of rhododendron is a priority, particularly in ancient woodlands that have been designated as Local Nature Reserves (LNRs). Buddleia is another invader, though it tends to be tolerated as its attraction to butterflies makes it an asset, as walkers through the Seaton valley will know!

Kilminorth Woods

Woodland path with bluebells, Kilminorth Woods

into their own, often found on dead timber, although wild mushrooms and toadstools can be found throughout the year. On the trees, bracket and porcelain fungi are common, and a wide range of species is found on or close to the woodland floor – honey fungus, chicken-in-the-woods, candle snuff, amethyst deceiver and many more.

Kilminorth Woods lie along the west bank of the West Looe River, and have been a LNR since 1993. Their 44 hectares are owned by Cornwall Council. They are easily accessible from Looe, and their network of signposted paths is popular with walkers and cyclists. They stretch in a narrow belt along the steep slopes of the river for about a mile and a half as far as the hamlet of Watergate. Within the woods there are occasional outcrops of the underlying Devonian slates, a reminder of the shallowness of the soil. Just up river from the main woodland entrance is a more open area with traces of an industrial past, known as the 'old boatyard'. This site was used for boatbuilding during the Second World War to supplement military production and operated until the 1990s. The site now provides a quite different habitat from the woodland proper, with grasses, gorse, willow and alder, and salt-tolerant species on the areas that flood. It is the best place in Kilminorth to see butterflies.

Kilminorth shows traces of human occupation much longer ago. The Giant's Hedge is a stone-faced earth bank, which may date from the sixth century, and probably demarcated the territory of a tribal chieftain. It originally extended from Looe for eight miles to Lerryn on the River Fowey; the section running through Kilminorth Woods is the longest that remains intact. It lies deep in the woodland and must have predated it. The bank is well preserved and is now topped in many places by mature trees, but it is most important for its abundance of bryophytes typical of western oak woods. It is excellent habitat for ground-dwelling small mammals like bank voles; it provides nest sites for robins and wrens, and a flight line for foraging bats.

Kilminorth is at present managed with a light touch by the Council, whose staff visit periodically to keep rides clear, maintain paths and steps, and are aided by the Friends of Kilminorth Woods, a group of local volunteers set up in 2006 to assist in the conservation of this precious asset.

Trenant Woods

Trenant Woods stand on the peninsula of land formed by the convergence of the two Looe rivers. Before they were acquired by the Woodland Trust in 1992, they had a chequered history. The townsfolk of Looe were outraged in the 1960s when a highly visible section of the woodland was felled. Initially the Woodland Trust purchased a narrow, V-shaped strip of land flanking the peninsula; this contained ASNW plus the clearings created by the felling. These were replanted in the 1990s, but leaving some open spaces. The area owned by the Trust has since more than doubled, with the purchase first of an area of grassland alongside the West Looe river, and then of a large tract of farmland within the 'V', where it has embarked on an exciting tree-planting project with the aim of creating a fully wooded peninsula. Thousands of trees have been planted, with a wide range of broad-leaved species, including oak, ash, holly, birch, rowan and wild cherry. It has not been plain sailing for the new woodland – deer have done a lot of damage to the young trees, and it has been necessary to construct a long, deer-proof fence to keep the marauders out. The grassland along the West Looe river is slowly being colonized with bramble, bracken and gorse.

Trenant Woods present a more varied ecological mosaic than Kilminorth, and their mixture of ASNW, new plantings, small clearings and rough grassland totals nearly 91 hectares. Skylarks, yellowhammers and meadow pipits are present in the more open areas. The woods are open to the public, but less accessible than Kilminorth, being approached by a long track from a parking area at Polpever. This is a place to enjoy solitude within sight of the busy town, but separated from it.

Seaton Valley

A few miles to the east, the steep-sided valley of the River Seaton, between Hessenford and the sea, is now both Country Park and LNR, and contains a third main area of valley woodlands, with a substantial amount

Autumn colours in Seaton Valley

Left to right: Golden-winged dragonfly attacking bumblebee; emperor dragonfly; long-winged coneheads

of ASNW. The character of Seaton Valley is quite different from the Looe valleys; it is not normally inundated at high tide, but the wet valley bottom contains grassy meadows, which sometimes flood, and three ponds. The meandering river has been straightened and modified over time, and cattle no longer graze the meadows. This site once housed a large caravan park. In parts of the valley floor, wet woodland has developed on the waterlogged ground, with plenty of alder and willow, and flowers like yellow flag iris and ragged robin flourish. Attempts are being made by local volunteers to check the encroachment on the open areas, to maintain habitats for butterflies. Seaton Valley is the most accessible of our three areas of valley woodland. A broad paved path runs north past the ponds, and in the upper part of the valley, a boardwalk (The Otter Trail)

follows the riverbank as far as the village of Hessenford.

The reed-fringed ponds provide a home for waterfowl, but are most noted for their dragonflies and damselflies. Most of Cornwall's dragonfly species can be seen here, and southern hawkers, golden-ringed dragonflies, common darters, emperor dragonflies and four-spotted chasers are regulars. Occasionally a rarer migrant dragonfly is recorded, like the yellow-winged darter in 1995. Dragonflies take their name from their aggressive appearance, and are top insect predators, feeding on other insects, especially flies, but sometimes bigger insects like bees and bumblebees. The wet ground is also attractive to amphibians like frogs and toads.

The more open areas of Seaton Valley are also good places to look for grasshoppers and crickets. In addition to the great green bush cricket (the UK's largest cricket), you may find the long-winged conehead, a species not recorded in Cornwall until 1990.

Kilminorth, Trenant and Seaton Valley contain the main areas of ASNW in the Looe area, but there are other patches of woodland in the river valleys. Upstream of Kilminorth there is wet woodland in the main valley floor; commercially managed woods of various types, including conifer plantations, flank the western side and extend up small tributary valleys. In the East Looe valley opposite Trenant lies more ASNW in the Morval estate south of Steppe's Pond. The corridors of woodland in these valleys are vitally important to the movement of wildlife.

Woodland mammals

The casual walker in the valley woodlands may well see a grey squirrel; other mammals are likely to remain out of sight, undetected. But if you are quiet and patient and early (or very late) you may be rewarded with the sighting of red fox, badger or roe deer. Of course, none of these animals are restricted

From top: Roe deer fawn; badgers; red fox

to woodland and all may be seen in other parts of the Looe area – deer particularly like to venture out into farmland to graze – and, sadly, all are frequent road casualties. The roe deer is the smallest of the indigenous deer species and is numerous. The West Looe valley is a good place to see them, especially at Watergate and along the grassland on the valley's eastern side, where they graze in the early morning. A local boatman reported seeing seven swimming together across the river.

The nocturnal badger is rarely seen in daylight hours, but there are signs of their presence throughout the woodlands – with many setts, some of which may be centuries old, plus tell-tale signs of their hair on fences, their latrines (badgers are fastidious about their toilet arrangements), and the scuffle marks on the woodland floor showing where they have rooted for food. The animals also venture out on to adjacent farmland, a good place for them to find one of their staple foods, earth worms. Foxes are common, and are seen sometimes on the riverbank at Watergate looking for an unwary water bird or rabbit.

But the most common mammal in these woodlands is rarely seen by visitors. We know of its abundance from small mammal surveys. A baited Longworth trap left overnight and checked the following morning is extremely likely to be occupied by a wood mouse. This tiny rodent lives mainly on the woodland floor, but as it is nocturnal we are rarely aware of its presence. These woods contain thousands of wood mice. But there are other rodents here too – bank voles, and common and pygmy shrews.

There is one rodent that is even more elusive – the hazel dormouse, one of Britain's endangered species. It is nocturnal, hibernates on the woodland floor in winter, and in summer may be high in the trees. It also tends to be present at relatively low densities. In Kilminorth local volunteers were encouraged to find out if dormice were resident in the woods. The signs were not propitious – Kilminorth does not have a great deal of hazel – but we now know that this species is more catholic in its choice of habitat than was previously thought. The presence of dormice can be detected by examining hazel nuts for signs of their distinctive dissection; the easier method is to place tubes in trees and hedges at low level in the hope that dormice will use them as temporary nest sites. Fifty tubes were sited in Kilminorth Woods, and

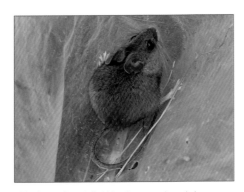

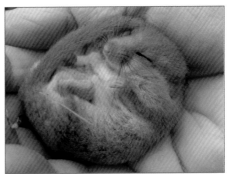

Clockwise from left: Wood mouse; hazel door-mouse; brown long-eared bat rescued in East Looe

in June 2011 the volunteers found what they were looking for – a beautifully constructed nest inside a tube. This was followed by an even clearer indication that dormice were present – a live animal scampered out of a tube and up a tree trunk. Since then, 50 dormouse boxes – more substantial structures – have been put in place, and patience was rewarded late in 2012 when two dormice were found. If dormice are present in Kilminorth, it is probable that they are also present in Trenant and other woodlands in the area – and in local hedgerows, and their presence has been confirmed in Seaton Valley. By law, dormouse boxes can only be checked by trained personnel with licences, so should you see one in these woodlands, please leave it alone.

There are other nocturnal mammals in the valley woodlands – members of the bat family. On summer evenings the woods are visited by pipistrelles, some streaming out from roofs in East Looe a few hundred metres away; brown long-eared bats, a common but often overlooked woodland species, have been found roosting in dormouse boxes. Brown long-eared bats also confirmed their presence in the locality when one ailing specimen needed rescue from a shop doorway in the main street in East Looe!

Woodland birds

The best time to discover woodland birds is spring, when birdsong at dawn gives reliable clues to the identity of the resident population. By mid-summer, when leaves are thick on the trees, sighting birds can be difficult.

The quintessential bird in these woodlands is the blue tit. We tend to think of this familiar species as a garden bird, but its true habitat is broad-leaved woodland. Erect a row of nest boxes in these woodlands, and most of them will be occupied by blue tits. In summer the birds feed high in the canopy on caterpillars, and time their nesting so that the feeding of the chicks coincides with the most productive period for this food source. They usually have only one brood for this reason.

But this is not the only member of the tit family to reside in these woods; great, long-tailed and coal tits are also common. The most unusual tit is the misleadingly named marsh tit, in fact a woodland species. It is a clean-cut, small tit with a black cap, and sometimes its presence can be detected by its explosive call, 'pichay'. This is one of the rarest bird species resident in the Looe area. It is red-listed in the UK, because its population has declined by over 50 per cent. Marsh tits breed in all three of our valley woodlands (sometimes in dormouse boxes!). In winter, they join locally with parties of tits wandering through the woodlands, perhaps in company with two other tiny residents – goldcrests and tree-creepers. Goldcrests are sometimes regarded as birds mainly of conifers, but they are common in these woods, in spring detected by their high-pitched song, but difficult to see as they move high in the canopy. In winter they are joined by birds that cross from the Continent, and occasionally by their flamboyant relative, the firecrest.

In spring, the woods resound with the repetitive song of the chiffchaff, while another member of the warbler family, the blackcap, projects its gorgeous rich notes from deep in cover. In Seaton Valley, in the wetter woodland, you may be lucky enough to hear the

 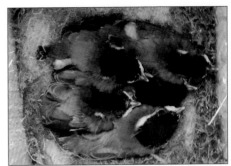

Blue tit in nest box (left). Young marsh tits occupy a dormouse box (right)

wistful declining cadence of the willow warbler. Throughout these woods you will hear the songs of wrens, robins and chaffinches. The familiar blackbird is a woodland species that is a garden favourite, and you also may hear the distinctive notes of Browning's 'wise (song) thrush' ('he sings each song twice over, Lest you should think he never could recapture The first fine careless rapture!') . The song thrush is no longer a common bird, and is also red-listed because of its steep decline. Early in the year the largest member of the thrush family, the mistle thrush, may also be heard, singing from the highest vantage point, sometimes in wild weather, earning its nickname the 'stormcock'.

Two of the most spectacular woodland breeding residents are the green and great spotted woodpecker. Both are betrayed by their call before you see them – the laughing 'yaffle' of the green, and the vibrant drumming of the great spotted. Great spotted woodpeckers are also frequent visitors to local garden birdfeeders. They are not averse to taking chicks of other birds, and sometimes enlarge the entrances to woodland nest boxes for this purpose. The best place to see the green woodpecker is not in the woods themselves but on adjacent grassland where it feeds on the ground on insects, especially ants. Another trunk-climbing species, the nuthatch, is a common and noisy resident; sometimes it nests in the boxes put up to monitor local populations, though usually customising them by adding sealants of mud cement.

Clockwise from top left: Great spotted woodpecker; green woodpecker and chick; song thrush; nuthatch

Among the larger woodland birds the wood pigeon is most numerous; its flimsy nests are common, and pairs often raise several broods. There are also members of the crow family – jays, jackdaws, ravens and crows. In the skies above the woodland, ravens sometimes joust with circling buzzards; both favour some of the largest trees in the woods for nesting. At night the woods echo with the hoots of resident tawny owls, which thrive on the abundance of small rodents.

Butterflies and moths

The dense canopy of the ASNW tends to restrict butterfly populations, as the ground flora is often sparse and lacks the food-plants to support them. Seaton Valley and Trenant, with more open areas, fare better than Kilminorth in this respect. Yet the spectacular silver-washed fritillary is found in all three woods. This large, strong-flying, orange and black butterfly takes its name from silver streaks on its hind-wing. It flies from July to September, feeding on nectar from brambles and aphid honeydew on tree leaves. The caterpillars feed on violet leaves. The most elusive butterfly in these woods is the purple hairstreak – this lives only in oak woods but feeds largely in the canopy and is frequently unobserved. The pretty little holly blue feeds on the abundant holly and ivy. Probably the commonest butterfly in the woods themselves is the speckled wood, but it is also possible to see peacocks, red admirals, gatekeepers and commas, and in the more open areas of grassland other butterflies flourish,

Sleepy tawny owl

including ringlets, meadow browns, skippers and the strikingly marked marbled white.

These woods come into their own for their moth populations. Set up a moth trap, and you are likely to attract a range of interesting specimens. The thousands of moth caterpillars found in oak woods are a vital food source for species higher up the food chain. The rarest moth found here is the Scarce Merveille du Jour, recorded in 2004 in Kilminorth Woods. It has been seen in a restricted area of a few trees. This is one of very few locations where it is found in Cornwall. With its

Clockwise from top left: Silver-washed fritillary; speckled wood; holly blue; scarce merveille du jour; purple hairstreak

marbled greenish-grey and black forewings, this beautiful creature is well camouflaged on tree trunks. It flies in June and July. Other relatively unusual moths found in this wood include the quaintly named bilberry pug, the waved carpet (rare in most of Britain) and the red-necked footman.

The Rural Hinterland: Farm, Field and Hedgerow

Behind the coast and between the river valleys there is a back country criss-crossed by flowery lanes and Cornish hedges, dotted with hamlets and scattered farms. This rural landscape is dominated by pastoral farming, though there are some arable fields too. Many farms, especially close to the coast, have taken on new functions associated with the holiday trade, as farmers supplement their income by running bed and breakfast, caravan and camping sites and riding facilities. In some small settlements like Trefanny Hill, Talehay and Treworgey, much of the property is now given over to holiday activity.

This landscape forms an important element of Wild Looe, and while much of the land is privately owned, plenty of footpaths provide access, and guests on farms have opportunities to see farm wildlife at first hand. Sadly some farmland is much less rich in wildlife than in the past. Where grassland has been 'improved' and traditional hay meadows replaced by silage, the high density of invertebrates and small rodents (especially field voles) that formerly characterized farmland has been lost, with serious consequences for those creatures higher up the food chain that depended on it for food supply. The removal of hedgerows to make bigger fields more suitable for machinery is another problem, reducing the habitat for many species.

Traditional Cornish hedges are a cherished feature of the landscape – usually stone-faced, decked with wildflowers, grasses and lichens, and home to a wide range of mammals, birds and invertebrates. Bank voles, rabbits, foxes and badgers are among those that make their home in these hedges. Rabbits are now back to perhaps half of the numbers found before the introduction of myxomatosis, and are sufficiently numerous to cause considerable damage to hedgerows with their pervasive burrowing. Rabbits are a staple food for buzzards, whose numbers have undoubtedly benefited from the recovery of the population. They are also prey for stoats, while the stoat's smaller cousin, the weasel, preys mainly on rodents. These tiny predators are most likely to be seen streaking across a secluded lane. The grasslands are also often riddled with molehills, though their creators are rarely seen.

In spring, primroses, red campions, lesser stitchworts, ramsons and many other flowering species produce a visual feast in hedges often capped with blossoming blackthorn and the 'may' of hawthorn. In summer, the lanes hum with insects, and here you will find yellowhammers, whitethroats and linnets singing from the hedge tops alongside the more familiar blackbirds, robins and wrens. Yellowhammers have declined greatly in numbers in many parts of England and are red-listed, but in the lanes around Pelynt and Lansallos they are still a common sight, and their persistent 'a little bit of bread and no cheeeese' remains a familiar sound. Many of the hedgerows are topped with trees and shrubs, providing more nesting sites for birds, and in harsh winters their berries become a magnet for flocks of redwings and fieldfares, beautiful visitors from the Continent. Sparrowhawks hunt for small birds along the hedges. One of the commonest hedgerow trees is the ash, and

Looe's rural hinterland, looking inland

Clockwise from top left: Stoat; mole – rarely seen at the surface; male yellowhammer

the impact of the ash dieback disease which invaded England in 2012 could be devastating for this landscape.

The farmhouses and farmyards of this area provide significant habitat for wildlife. While the brown rats and large flocks of wintering starlings may not be welcome, other species are cherished. On dairy farms the herds of cattle attract insects, and insects attract swallows. The barns on a large dairy farm like

Trenake near Pelynt provide nest sites for colonies of this favourite summer visitor, with more than a dozen pairs on a single farm. The farms remain strongholds for house sparrows too, now a scarce sight in more urban locations, and a few also have small colonies of another attractive summer visitor, the house martin. Many farms have preserved or remade ponds, adding greatly to their biodiversity. Swallows and martins hawk for flies over the water; moorhens and little grebes dive for food, and damselflies and dragonflies abound. Canada geese – those prolific colonists of the British countryside – are regular breeders at many of these scattered water bodies, and may be less welcome. Some larger ponds are given over to recreational fishing. At Bake Lakes in the east

Clockwise from top left: Swallow; mature ash trees line a Cornish hedge at West Muchlarnick; primroses in a hedgerow

of our area, a series of large fishing ponds is one of the best places to see dragonflies and damselflies, and the stocks of fish inevitably attract herons and kingfishers.

The availability of rodents as prey for owls is vital, and it is heartening that barn owls remain a part of the rural hinterland's 'birdscape'. This species has suffered greatly in Britain from grassland improvement, as its main prey is the field vole. This small rodent needs unimproved, tussocky grassland. Barn owls have also declined elsewhere because of the loss of accessible nest sites in old barns, and from the depredations of poisons and speeding traffic. Only one in 75 farms in Britain still has nesting barn owls, a shocking statistic. But in Wild Looe's rural hinterland there are still places where you have a rea-

The ancient pattern of small fields at West Muchlarnick

sonable chance of watching a barn owl hunting along hedges and across fields of unimproved grassland. Provision of nest boxes at some sites has attracted breeding birds.

Some farms buck the trend, and have retained the traditional landscape with little concession to field enlargement and other aspects of modernization such as the application of chemical fertilizers. One such example is West Muchlarnick, recently bequeathed to the CWT. Its previous owner had largely kept the pattern of small fields, fringed by thick hedges and sunken tracks. The field pattern has changed little since the 1840s, and there are more than five kilometres of hedgerows. The CWT has begun

Wildflower meadow at Penadlake (left). Early marsh orchids (right)

a programme of hedgerow restoration to maintain the farm's traditional character, and has introduced small numbers of traditional breeds of sheep and cattle, Dorset Downs and Devon Ruby Reds.

At Penadlake near Lanreath, Philip Hambly has gone a stage further, developing a stunning landscape of wildflower meadows, broad-leaved woodland and lily ponds in an attempt to create a more wildlife-friendly area. Already this habitat is rich with a wide range of species – marsh tits, great spotted woodpeckers and purple hairstreaks in the woodland; little grebes, lilies, flag irises and dragonflies on the ponds; yellow rattle, sorrel, ox-eye daisies and clover in the drier meadows, with a kaleidoscope of colours evolving through the seasons. The wet meadows within the woodland display an amazing array of flowers, with hundreds of early marsh orchids, and a profusion of ragged robins, forget-me-nots, buttercups and other plants relishing the damp environment. Orange tips, peacocks, green-veined whites and many other butterflies flutter

Snipe: a study in camouflage

across the landscape. In summer families of tufted ducks, mallards and moorhens scuttle across the water. Here too you may be lucky enough to find the spotted flycatcher, in one of its last footholds in south-east Cornwall. This delightful summer visitor has declined catastrophically in southern England. In spring, the woodland rings with the song of blackcaps and willow warblers and the drumming of woodpeckers, while the jangling notes of sedge warblers can be heard from the reeds fringing the ponds. In winter, flocks of finches are attracted to strips of seed-bearing crops and highly-camouflaged snipe lurk in the reeds. A visit to Lethytep at Penadlake (open to the public for a few days in summer) is truly inspirational, and a reminder of what too much of the British countryside has lost.

The crow family

'Seagulls' are a ubiquitous presence in the Looe area, but there is another family of birds that vies with it in numbers and whose members are found everywhere in the locality, particularly in the rural hinterland. While members of the gull family are predominantly white, members of this family are predominantly black. Look up in the sky, along the shore, or across rooftops, woods or fields, and you are certain before long to see crows. Like gulls, crows are not always popular – they are scavengers and robbers – but like gulls they are resourceful, adaptable and clever – hence their abundance.

In the Looe area there are six members of the crow family. The jay is the most specialized – essentially a woodland bird with a particular liking for oaks where it feeds on acorns. Its raucous alarm call is often heard before the white rump of the bird signals its departure. Magpies, brash and noisy, are birds of the hedgerow, copse and open fields, and can be seen throughout the area's countryside. The powerful raven is a carrion eater that thrives in sheep country and breeds on cliffs along the Looe coast, as well as in the valley woodlands. Its deep croak as

Rookery in West Looe (top). Carrion crow (left).
Jay (above)

it soars overhead betrays its presence. The much smaller jackdaw is ubiquitous; it is a common urban bird, often nesting in roofs and chimneys. It is also a bird of the country-side, often nesting in farm buildings.

But rooks are the most numerous 'crow' around Looe. They are birds of farmland, where they feed on the ground, using their powerful beaks to probe for invertebrates. They nest colonially in rookeries sited high in mature trees. The biggest rookery in the Looe area is actually in the town, in the trees on either side of the Polperro Road, whose residents wake in spring to a cacophony of cawing. There are over 100 nests in this rookery, and for a few weeks each year the sky above the Polperro Road becomes a busy flyway of rooks heading out to gather food in the fields. However, there were bigger rook-eries in the area in the past. The rookery at Trelawne Manor west of Looe was once the largest in Cornwall. In 1847 the Polperro doctor Jonathan Couch instructed his patient Lewis Harding to convalesce by making daily records of the Trelawne rookery for a year. Harding counted an extraordinary 478 nests, all completed by mid-April. The Trelawne rookery still exists in the trees at the entrance to the modern holiday park, but with only 60 nests in 2012. Looe Bay Holiday Park to the east of the town also has a substantial rook-ery, with many of the nests in large conifers, and there are rookeries at several other sites.

Rooks and carrion crows are commonly confused, though their beaks are quite differ-ent, and country lore stresses the solitariness of crows and the gregariousness of rooks. It is true that carrion crows tend to nest in iso-lation, but it is not unusual to see groups of crows, especially feeding at low tide on the mud of the Looe rivers. The collective term for a group of crows is a 'murder' – not inap-propriate in view of their habits.

Sadly, a seventh member of the crow fam-ily is missing in the Looe area. The red-billed chough is Cornwall's bird, appearing on its coat of arms, but for many years it did not breed in the county. Jonathan Couch report-ed that choughs had become rare around Polperro in the 1840s, and the last breeding pair may have been the birds he recorded on the cliffs at Lizzen in 1857, which successfully raised three young. Choughs have now re-turned to breed in small numbers on cliffs in west and north Cornwall. They like to forage for invertebrates on grassy cliff tops grazed by cattle. There is potentially suitable habitat in the Looe-Polperro area, so hope remains that they may one day return.

Postscript: A Wheatear on the Roof

One spring morning a couple of years ago I drew back my bedroom curtains and found an exhausted wheatear sitting forlornly on the conservatory roof. It had presumably just crossed the Channel on its way north. The wheatear is essentially a moorland bird but passes through south Cornwall in March – usually the earliest returning migrant and a cheering harbinger of summer. My bird spent a couple of hours resting in the sunshine and then it was on its way. Such serendipitous encounters live in the memory.

They are also a reminder that even if you stay at home, wildlife will come to you. We end where we began, with the potential everyday experience of the town dwellers of Looe. The wild side of Looe or Polperro is literally on one's doorstep. From my suburban window I constantly see gulls overhead – but also crows plus the occasional buzzard or sparrowhawk and sometimes, in summer, swifts – while those who live in the older, more densely built parts of these towns, have jackdaws and pigeons as well as gulls sharing their accommodation.

A wheatear on my roof

Gardens are havens for wildlife, encouraged by the presence of food and shelter. They remain the best place to see the worryingly scarce hedgehog, now in catastrophic decline. The relative absence of hedgehog corpses on our roads may seem to be a good thing, but is an indication of a relative absence of these delightful creatures, whose numbers have declined dramatically – by a third since 2000. Friends in West Looe are regularly visited by badgers, which enjoy